T0295831

Effective Workforce Development

Developed for busy HR practitioners and trainers, this book provides a concise guide to the theory and practice of employee training in contemporary organisations. Reflecting the importance of employee development to learning-based organisations in the knowledge economy, it clearly links employee training needs to business development and offers an accessible guide to current theories combined with research-based practical guidance in how to design effective training programmes.

Covering all the current theories about training and development and the latest thinking about workplace learning interventions, this concise, practical guide will be an essential source for HR practitioners and line managers seeking to improve organisational learning and performance.

Dr Antonios Panagiotakopoulos holds a PhD in Human Resource Management from the University of Leeds, where he serves as a Research Fellow and Dissertation Tutor at the Centre for Employment Relations, Innovation and Change (CERIC). He has previously worked as a Lecturer in HRM teaching courses at Leeds University and Chester University, as well as a Senior Lecturer of HRM in several Higher Education Institutions in Greece (e.g. New York College, Athens and American College of Greece). During his career he has won several teaching and research awards, while his articles have been published in various international peer-reviewed academic journals including *International Journal of Training and Development*, *Journal of Business Strategy*, and *The Learning Organization*.

Routledge Focus on Business and Management

The fields of business and management have grown exponentially as areas of research and education. This growth presents challenges for readers trying to keep up with the latest important insights. Routledge Focus on Business and Management presents small books on big topics and how they intersect with the world of business research.

Individually, each title in the series provides coverage of a key academic topic, whilst collectively, the series forms a comprehensive collection across the business disciplines.

Liminality in Organization Studies
Theory and Method
Maria Rita Tagliaventi

Branding and Positioning in Base of Pyramid Markets in Africa
Innovative Approaches
Charles Blankson, Stanley Coffie and Joseph Darmoe

Ephemeral Retailing
Pop-up Stores in a Postmodern Consumption Era
Ghalia Boustani

Effective Workforce Development
A Concise Guide for HR and Line Managers
Antonios Panagiotakopoulos

Employment Relations and Ethnic Minority Enterprise
An Ethnography of Chinese Restaurants in the UK
Xisi Li

For more information about this series, please visit: www.routledge.com/ Routledge-Focus-on-Business-and-Management/book-series/FBM

Effective Workforce Development

A Concise Guide for HR and Line Managers

Antonios Panagiotakopoulos

Routledge
Taylor & Francis Group

LONDON AND NEW YORK

First published 2020
by Routledge
2 Park Square, Milton Park, Abingdon, Oxon OX14 4RN

and by Routledge
52 Vanderbilt Avenue, New York, NY 10017

Routledge is an imprint of the Taylor & Francis Group, an informa business

© 2020 Antonios Panagiotakopoulos

British Library Cataloguing-in-Publication Data
A catalogue record for this book is available from the British Library

Library of Congress Cataloging-in-Publication Data
A catalog record has been requested for this book

ISBN: 978-0-367-33250-1 (hbk)
ISBN: 978-0-429-31887-0 (ebk)

Typeset in Times New Roman
by Wearset Ltd, Boldon, Tyne and Wear

Contents

Acknowledgements

This book is dedicated to Maria. Her endless love, encouragement and support have been of the utmost importance for me. I extend my sincere thanks to my parents, my sister and her family, Maria's grandparents and a few close friends for their continuous encouragement. My mentors at the University of Leeds, Professor Mark Stuart and Professor Christopher Forde, also deserve my special thanks for their valuable guidance during my entire academic career. Last but not least, I would like to thank Jacqueline Curthoys at Routledge for supporting this effort with so much enthusiasm.

Aims of the book

As the title suggests, this book provides – in an easy-to-digest format – a very comprehensive analysis to employee training and learning at work for busy HR professionals and other line managers concerned with developing employee skills. Essentially, it aims to provide the busy manager with an understanding not only of the potential of systematic training and informal on-the-job learning to contribute to improved organisational performance and individual well-being at work but also why it very often fails to yield such positive outcomes. The ultimate aim of this book is to raise the awareness of HR and line managers on how to create the necessary conditions at work in order to unleash human talent that will drive organisational success.

About the author

Dr Antonios Panagiotakopoulos holds a PhD in Human Resource Management from the University of Leeds, where he serves as a Research Fellow and Dissertation Tutor at the Centre for Employment Relations, Innovation and Change (CERIC). He has previously worked as a Lecturer in HRM teaching courses at Leeds University and Chester University, as well as a Senior Lecturer of HRM in several Higher Education Institutions in Greece (e.g. New York College, Athens and American College of Greece). During his career he has won several teaching and research awards, while his articles have been published in various international peer-reviewed academic journals including *International Journal of Training and Development*, *Journal of Business Strategy* and *The Learning Organization*.

Introduction

The emergence of the knowledge-based society

The business environment is becoming more complex and more competitive. Organisations of all types are faced with a number of challenges presented by a fast-paced, highly dynamic and global economy. To survive and thrive in this environment, today's organisations must be even more competitive and adaptive and, what is more, must foster quality, cost reduction and innovation. To accomplish these goals, organisations have to ensure both the willingness and ability of their staff to meet all these targets.

The rate of technological change is now greater than it has ever been and for that reason organisations not only need to train their employees but also to help them learn faster than their competitors. Human resource training activities can be used to ensure that the members of organisations have what it takes to successfully meet their challenges. In the new knowledge-based economy, the most important intellectual property is what is inside employees' heads. As several academics and business leaders have noted, managers will always have to find ways of developing and mobilising the intelligence, knowledge and creative potential of human beings at every level of the organisation and become increasingly skilled in placing quality people in key places and developing their full potential. It will become increasingly important to recruit people who enjoy learning and relish change, as well as to motivate employees to be intelligent, flexible and adaptive.

Across the industrialised world and in many developing countries too, it is argued that workforce education and training are the answer to numerous economic and social problems, ranging from competitiveness, productivity and economic growth to unemployment and social exclusion. At the same time, there has been a broad range of criticisms about the limitations of such an approach, which rests on the simplistic argument that better training systems give rise to better economic performance. It should be noted that within each society the relationship between human resource development (HRD) and economic performance is shaped by broader institutional structures such as government organisations, labour market regulation, the education and training system, the financial and banking system and the industrial relations system, within all of which the process of skills formation is embedded. Education and training are important factors in economic success but there are numerous other factors linked to economic growth.

Despite the scepticism about heavy reliance on education and training to resolve social and economic problems, it is still the case that the claims about the vital role of well-trained, high-skilled and high-productivity labour to ensure living standards in the advanced countries are to be sustained and improved, are realistic. The challenges posed by the rise of low-cost producers in other parts of the world can be met only if labour in the advanced countries has high levels of skills, which will differentiate it from the capacities of workers in the newly industrialising countries. Productivity gains and innovation cannot be achieved on the basis of low-skilled work. Most countries in Europe are facing the challenges of competition and quality and, hence, they need a high-skills base in their economies.

In the global economy, capital and finance are increasingly easily transferred. It is the human resource which therefore becomes the major difference between competing economies. Workforce training is essential to equip employees with the skills required to make themselves more productive and adaptable. When tastes and technologies are changing rapidly, necessitating a high rate of labour turnover across industries and occupations, adaptability is crucial for keeping labour employed and maintaining competitiveness. Beyond that, without a workforce that is continuously acquiring new skills, managers are not able to introduce more sophisticated and productive machines and, thus, it becomes difficult to reap most of the returns from technological advances.

Employee training defined

Workforce development is defined broadly as a set of activities designed by an organisation to provide its members with the opportunities to learn necessary skills to meet current job demands and prepare them for future job responsibilities. To put it simply, human resource training comprises the procedures and processes that purposively seek to provide learning activities to enhance the skills, knowledge and capabilities of people, teams and the organisation so that there is a change in action to achieve the desired outcomes. Its focus is on changing or improving the knowledge, skills and attitudes of individuals. There is a sort of distinction between the terms 'training' and 'development'. *Training* represents activities that teach employees how to better perform their present jobs while *development* involves those activities that prepare an employee for future responsibilities. Although the emphasis of this publication is on training, it should be stressed that the distinction between training and development is often blurred and primarily one of intent. At the heart of training and development is human learning.

Aims of employee training

The overall aim of human resource training is to ensure that the organisation has the quality of people it needs to achieve its objectives for improved performance and growth. After a job placement, many employees may not have the ability to perform well in their new job. Often they must be trained in the duties they are expected to do. Even if they are experienced workers, they must be trained in order to learn about the organisation and its culture, to be able to work effectively with new workmates, to enhance their existing skills and to improve their performance. In addition, existing employees need to be trained in order to achieve and sustain superior performance. However, it should be pointed out that training does more than just prepare employees to perform their jobs effectively. Training for special purposes – dealing with AIDS in the workplace and adjusting to workforce diversity, for example – is also required in order to help employees become aware of and cope with such issues. On the other hand, the long-term development of human resources – as distinct from training – reduces the company's dependence on hiring new workers. If employees are developed properly, then new job openings are likely to be filled internally. Furthermore, promotions and transfers facilitate the achievement of employee career goals and employees, in turn, feel a greater commitment to the firm and work towards the achievement of strategic business objectives. Generally, the ultimate objective of most, if not all, human resource training programmes is to improve organisational performance.

1 The learning process

The learning cycle

Learning is a process by which human beings become aware of themselves and their environment through the acquisition of knowledge, understanding, skills and values in order to control or adapt to their environment, grow and prosper. The learning process engages an individual's emotional and intellectual dimensions and involves change of a relatively permanent nature. In the following paragraphs, a comprehensive analysis will be presented on how people learn.

Human learning is a complex process, and is affected by a host of internal (i.e. the individual) and external (i.e. the context of learning) factors. The internal factors include an individual's cognitive ability, personal values, emotional state, physical health, motivation and previous learning experience. On the other hand, external factors include the trainer's ability to teach, the physical learning environment, the different learning aids and provision of quality feedback.

One of the most influential ideas about human learning came from David Kolb in his book on the subject of experiential learning, published in 1984. Experiential Learning Theory (ELT) essentially provides a holistic model of the learning process and is a multi-linear model of adult development, both of which are consistent with what we know about how we naturally learn, grow and develop. The theory emphasises the pivotal role that experience plays in the learning process. The basic model is shown in Figure 1.1.

As can be seen in Kolb's cycle, the starting point of the learning process is a concrete experience of some kind – for example, using a calculator for the first time. Following this experience the trainee makes a number of observations (e.g. about the layout of buttons) and begins to formulate abstract concepts. These concepts are then tested in a new situation (e.g. by practising on the buttons). The practice itself provides a new experience

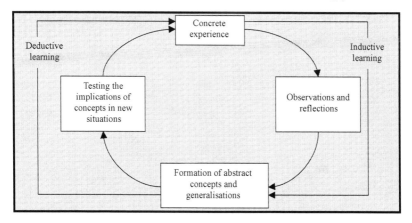

Figure 1.1 The experiential learning cycle (Kolb, D.).
Source: Adapted from Kolb, D. A., Rubin, I. M. and McIntyre, J. M. (1974) *Organizational Psychology: An experiential approach.* 2nd edn. Prentice Hall, p. 28.

and the learning cycle begins again. Kolb's cycle encompasses both inductive and deductive learning. Inductive learning is the process in which the learner may experience an event and draw a conclusion from it, while deductive learning starts with a theory, which is then applied by the learner. In short, Kolb's learning cycle stresses that effective learning requires the involvement of the learner at four levels: feeling (i.e. experiencing), observing, thinking and doing.

It can be seen from this learning cycle that learning is more than just applying rules or responding to small-scale problems. Learning is about developing insight and understanding and making complex connections between the key elements of a subject. It is a process that involves mental mapping, problem-solving skills, perceptions and motivation.

Learning styles

Based on the above-mentioned learning cycle several authors attempted in the past to identify different learning styles so that suitable learning interventions could be designed. One of the most popular frameworks for the analysis of learning styles was developed by Honey and Mumford in 1982. The four different styles created are as follows:

1   *Activists:* These persons learn through activity and challenging tasks, whereas they get bored with too much theory.

2   *Reflectors:* These are thoughtful individuals who enjoy participating in concrete experiences but then wish to reflect on them and puzzle things out.
3   *Theorists:* These are logical thinkers who try to create an integrated explanation (theory) based on observation.
4   *Pragmatists:* These are action-oriented individuals who enjoy putting ideas into practice. These learners like taking ideas from their theoretical standpoint and testing them in practice.

Learning principles

Based on the writings of well-known authors in the field of adult learning such as David Kolb and Carl Rogers, several conclusions on how people learn have been drawn. The most important adult learning principles are presented briefly below.

- Human beings have a natural potentiality for learning (i.e. they are curious). Therefore, the role of facilitators in learning is to provide an encouraging climate for learning, to help people clarify their goals and build on their own motivation, to make a wide range of learning resources available, to accept feelings in the learning process and to share knowledge in the learning process with their learners.
- Significant learning takes place when the subject-matter is deemed as highly relevant to the learner.
- Much learning takes place by doing. Learning is facilitated when the learner participates actively in the learning process.
- Independence, creativity and self-reliance are all facilitated when self-criticism and self-evaluation are in place rather than external assessment.
- Feedback on the progress of learning is vital for the learner in order to adjust their behaviour to meet desirable performance targets. Without feedback, learners have no basis for a change in their behaviour.
- Repetition is important in the process of learning. It is well known that learners' performance improves when they practise doing the same things over and over. This is related to the way in which cells in the human brain communicate, and the physical changes that they undergo when they communicate repeatedly as people continue practising the same action.
- The lesser the gap between the training intervention and the job, the greater the possibility of knowledge transfer. If employees are unable to transfer their learning to the work context because they are not able to retain all the training information, then the training effort may have been wasted.

- Reinforcement is critical in learning. It is the strengthening of a behaviour. It occurs in learning when a reward follows the behaviour. To increase the probability that the behaviour will be repeated, the reward must be seen as a consequence of the behaviour. Rewards can be tangible or psychological.

All the aforementioned learning principles should be taken into consideration by trainers and line managers when the stage of designing training interventions is reached, in order to maximise employee learning.

2 Training and organisational performance

Impact of training on organisational performance

As mentioned in the foreword of this book, employee training is an important activity that offers a number of benefits to organisations and individuals. Today, it is employee know-how that represents a key source of sustainable competitive advantage. There is already extensive literature indicating that training can help firms to improve employee performance and it is therefore a key element of organisational success. More specifically, workforce skills development usually leads to: increased productivity; increased job satisfaction; improved employee confidence and morale; enhanced employee commitment and loyalty since it reinforces their perceptions that the organisation is a good place in which to work; more effective decision-making and problem-solving; reduced stress; and improved organisational climate. Furthermore, in the existing era of increasingly precarious employment around the globe, it serves as an important mechanism of job security for employees since it improves their employability. In addition, training helps the people of an organisation to understand their customers' needs and therefore work towards satisfying them. This role of training is vital for the success of an organisation since the success of an organisation is based not only on the loyalty and commitment of the employees but also on their awareness of the customers' expectations. Last but not least, it improves communication between groups and builds team cohesiveness. In Table 2.1, a detailed list of the benefits of training for individuals and organisations is presented based on the findings from various research studies that have been conducted during the last few decades in the field of human resource development (HRD).

However, although employee training is important, it should be pointed out that without Senior Management and employee support and commitment to training, the major focus of an organisation is likely to be on activities other than training. Top management and employee cooperation and

Table 2.1 Benefits of employee training

- Through training, motivational variables of recognition, achievement, growth, responsibility and advancement are internalised and operationalised
- Aids in encouraging and achieving self-development and self-confidence
- Increases job satisfaction
- Improves job security (fosters employability)
- Helps create a better corporate image (positive impact on sales, as well as on attracting high-calibre staff)
- Improves staff loyalty
- Reduces accident rates at work
- Aids in understanding and carrying out organisational policies
- Provides information for future needs in all areas of the organisation
- Organisation benefits from more effective decision-making and problem-solving
- Aids in development for promotion from within
- Aids in developing various soft skills that successful workers usually display
- Aids in increasing productivity and quality of work
- Improves customer service quality
- Helps keep costs down in many areas (e.g. reduced error rates)
- Improves labour-management relations (improved inter-personal communication)
- Helps employees adjust to change
- Helps eliminate fear in attempting new tasks
- Aids in handling conflict, thereby helping to prevent stress and tension
- Builds cohesiveness in groups
- Aids in orientation for new employees and those taking new jobs through transfer or promotion

mutual contribution are prerequisites for the training interventions in order to benefit the organisation and the individuals concerned. In this context, employees must be well informed by the human resource development professionals about the importance and benefits of the training activity in order to be motivated to participate actively in this process. Employees need to be ready to learn and human resource managers need to know the factors affecting employee behaviour so that they can encourage and motivate their employees continually. Such factors involve the general state of the economy, technological changes, the work environment, employee motivation to learn, knowledge and skills already possessed by employees, etc. For example, technological changes impact on employee behaviour since technology creates redundancies and employee obsolescence, making employees require ongoing training to acquire new, marketable skills.

Barriers to training

In the existing HRD literature, several barriers to formal and informal training have been identified to date including financial and time constraints, lack of management commitment, low-cost business strategies, poor job design, lack of awareness around the importance of training, and 'poaching concerns'. Among the aforementioned barriers, staff poaching features in several research studies as one of the major barriers to training especially when it comes to small enterprises. Staff poaching is defined as the process of attracting employees of another company. To put it simply, staff poaching is the process through which a company hires an employee from a competing company. This is a phenomenon that adversely affects significantly smaller firms that are not in a position to offer generous rewards or any promotional opportunities in order to keep their well-trained employees. Employee poaching is considered by larger firms as a cost-effective means of attracting high-skilled employees since they can avoid the cost of training provision.

However, it should be stressed that such poaching can be reduced in cases where firms provide incentives to trained workers to stay with the firm after training is completed. Such incentives may include various financial and non-financial rewards. For example, small enterprises may offer a range of non-financial rewards (with no impact on their limited budget) including a harmonious working climate, employee involvement in decision-making, more varied job tasks and work flexibility to encourage well-trained staff to remain in the company. It is therefore important for HR and other line managers to recognise that a holistic HR approach to the development of employees is needed to retain their human talents so that they are not discouraged from designing training interventions to develop the capacities of their staff. It is also important for managers to remember that the cost of having poorly trained staff can be higher for the organisation in the long term than the cost of training provision. Many managers keep saying: What if I train my staff and then they go to work for our competitors? However, at the same time, they should ask themselves: What if I do not train them and they stay in the company?

Human resource training policy

Human resource management (HRM) policies are statements which assist in the guidance of decision-making and are communicated to all employees, usually in writing. In a similar manner, the training policy statement of an organisation sets out what the organisation is prepared to do in terms of developing its employees. It is important for organisations to have a human resource training policy because it reassures employees that they will be treated fairly as far as it concerns their learning opportunities, and, also, it helps managers to make quick decisions concerning training issues, as well as defend them. For example, the statement:

> *'The bank is fully aware of the need to provide the members of its staff with good opportunities for career development by offering them the opportunity for promotion to higher grades in line with their length of service and to rise to posts of responsibility in line with their professional expertise, skills and desires, as well as the Bank's operational requirements',*

gives a clear guideline to managers and employees about how promotional opportunities will be handled within the specific organisation.

Strategic employee training

Employee training must be aligned with business objectives in order to have a positive impact on the organisation's ability to compete. This means that human resource training policies, plans, procedures and practices should be linked to corporate goals if an organisation is to gain any real benefit from training expenditure. The ultimate aim of employee training is to help organisations and individuals to compete more effectively now and in the future. It involves a strategic, long-term and systematic way of thinking about people. A strategic human resource training approach aims to meet an organisation's specific business objectives and concentrates on the long term, which means that micro-environmental, as well as macro-environmental influences that will impact on the organisation, should be taken into account. As can be seen in Figure 2.1, both the macro-environment of the organisation, which involves political, economic, legal, socio-cultural, technological, and environmental factors, and its micro-environment, which encompasses suppliers, competitors, customers, employees, shareholders, available budget, corporate culture, and company size and structure, determine the corporate strategic plan (i.e. mission statement, objectives and overall strategy of the organisation). The human resource training activity of the organisation is heavily influenced, in turn, by the organisation's strategic plan.

For example, changes in technology may force an organisation to set customer service improvement as a strategic business objective. This means that human resource training activity must address this aim. Otherwise, the organisation's business strategy will not be supported and training interventions will take place just for their own sake, ending up quite frequently being a waste of time and money.

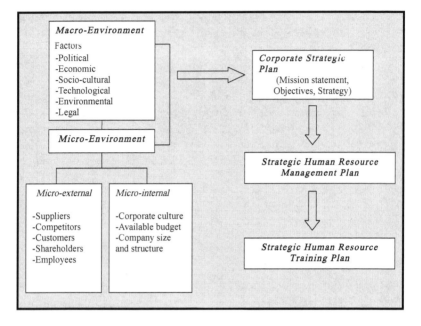

Figure 2.1 Strategic human resource training process.

Source: Adapted from (a) Delahaye, B. L. (2000) *Human Resource Development*. John Wiley & Sons Australia, p. 89; and (b) Reid, M. A., Barrington, H. and Brown, M. (2004) *Human Resource Development: Beyond training interventions*, 7th edn. London: CIPD, p. 93.

The link of employee training to other human resource management activities

Human resource management involves the acquisition, development, reward and motivation, maintenance and departure of an organisation's human resources. There are a number of human resource management activities that must be undertaken to satisfy the above aims including employee selection, training, performance evaluation and rewards. Each activity and function is inter-related and together they represent the core of human resource management (Figure 2.2). As it can be seen in the figure, employee training represents one of the three areas of the HRD function.

The human resource training activity is inter-related with all of the human resource management functions. For example, it is inter-related with staff recruitment and selection. The quality of employees who will be recruited to join an organisation is a crucial factor that affects the training activity within an organisation, since well-qualified employees need less training and expect quicker development in order to meet their career

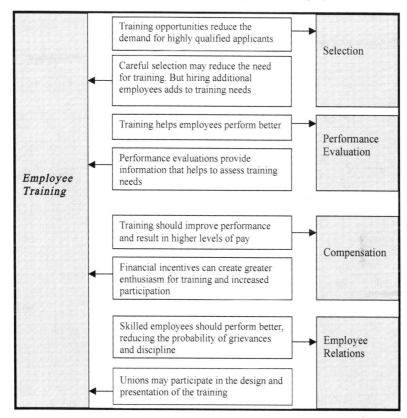

Figure 2.2 The interaction between training and other HRM activities.
Source: Adapted from Cherrington, D. J. (1995) *The Management of Human Resources*, 4th edn. New Jersey: Prentice Hall, p. 322.

expectations while less-well-qualified workers need much more training. It is also linked with the human resource performance appraisal activity since performance appraisal reveals the areas in which individual employees have poor performance and need to be trained. The above inter-relationship is presented diagrammatically in Figure 2.3.

The conclusion which is drawn from the above discussion is that employee training activity must be a part of a co-ordinated effort to improve the productive contribution of people in meeting the organisation's strategic business objectives. Changes in just one part of the HRM function are unlikely to bring the desired results in terms of organisational performance.

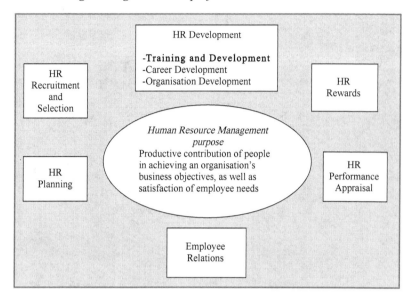

Figure 2.3 The Human Resource Management (HRM) function.

Source: Adapted from DeSimone, R. L., Werner, J. M. and Harris, D. M. (2002) *Human Resource Development*, 3rd edn. Fort Worth: Harcourt College Publishers, pp. 8–9.

3 The systematic approach to employee training

The systematic training model

Training is an investment in the human 'capital' of the organisation. It is essential to measure the adequacy of the 'return on investment' for training efforts. The return is likely to be higher if a systematic approach to training and development is taken rather than a random one since this permits the HR manager to design proper training interventions that address specific organisational problems, as well as demonstrate how employee training contributes to the organisation's strategic business objectives. A systematic human resource training process model involves a four-step sequence: needs analysis, design, implementation and evaluation. These phases of the training process are presented in the following paragraphs.

Training activities begin when a new employee enters the organisation, usually in the form of employee orientation. Thereafter, a four-phase systematic training model is widely used by a number of authors and researchers in the human resource management field, which is also known as the human resource training cycle. The four-step model involves the following (Figure 3.1):

1 *The assessment of training needs*
2 *The design of training activity*
3 *The implementation of training activity*
4 *The evaluation of training activity.*

Employee orientation

Employee orientation (or induction/initial training) is a key part of the training activity. Essentially, it is the process by which new employees learn important organisational values and norms, establish working relationships and learn how to function within their jobs. The systematic introduction of the new employees to their jobs, colleagues and the organisation is essential

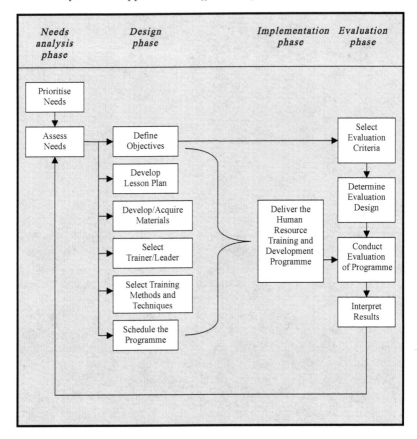

Figure 3.1 The systematic training model.

Source: Adapted from DeSimone, R. L., Werner, J. M. and Harris, D. M. (2002) *Human Resource Development*, 3rd edn. Fort Worth: Harcourt College Publishers, p. 127.

Table 3.1 Benefits of employee orientation

- Eliminates the stress of newcomers
- Fosters positives attitudes and job satisfaction
- Fosters a sense of commitment at the start of employment
- Makes the new employees feel bonded to the organisation early
- Reduces labour turnover
- Improves organisational profitability and competitiveness
- Achieves significant cost savings

and provides a number of benefits to the organisation and the individual (Table 3.1).

The content of the orientation programme often includes learning about the organisation (e.g. its goals, values and policies), learning to function in the work group (e.g. norms, roles and friendships within the group) and learning about the job (e.g. how to perform it, duties and responsibilities). An orientation checklist is presented in Table 3.2.

Table 3.2 Indicative employee orientation checklist

Company overview	• History
	• Values, mission, strategic business objectives
	• Key personnel
	• Products and services
Health and safety	• Medical examination
	• First aid
	• Safety equipment
	• Sexual harassment
	• Smoking
	• Substance abuse
	• Workplace violence
Employee relations	• Terms and conditions of employment
	• Probationary period
	• Performance appraisal
	• Lateness/absenteeism/sickness
	• Discipline
	• Grievance procedures
	• Dress code
	• Employee privacy
	• Training and development
Job description	• Responsibilities
	• Performance expectations
	• Reporting relationships
	• Assistance available
Compensation	• Pay
	• Overtime
	• Holiday pay
Facilities	• Rest rooms
	• Cafeteria
	• Car Parking
Benefits	• Medical insurance
	• Life insurance
	• Holidays
	• Special leave
	• Superannuation
Introductions	• Mentor
	• Union representative
	• Colleagues
	• Key Managers

The main training techniques that can be used during employee orientation involve either formal learning interventions such as video presentations, manuals, and audio material and/or informal approaches such as intensive coaching by more senior experienced staff. An essential part of the employee orientation process is the interview of newcomers with their supervisor that must be followed after delivery of the orientation programme ('follow-up') in order to ensure that there are no unanswered questions and misunderstandings. The worst mistake a company can make is to ignore the new employee after orientation. Therefore, many of the topics covered during orientation will need to be explained briefly again, once the employee has had the opportunity to experience them first-hand.

The assessment phase

Needs assessment is a process by which an organisation's human resource training and needs are identified and translated into training objectives. This stage is partly concerned with defining the gap between what is happening and what should happen (Figure 3.2). This gap is what has to be filled by training, i.e. the difference between what people know and can do and what they should know and be able to do in order to achieve the organisation's goals. Furthermore, this phase can reveal any future training needs – that is, the range of skills that employees need to acquire so that the company can stay ahead of competition in the future (i.e. proactive approach to training).

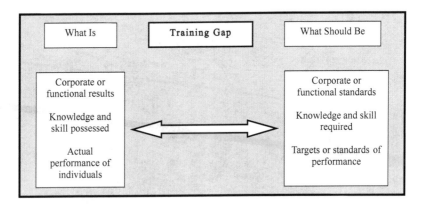

Figure 3.2 The training gap.
Source: Adapted from Armstrong, M. (1999) *A Handbook of Human Resource Management Practice*, 7th edn. London: Kogan Page, p. 514.

In other words, the needs assessment phase establishes what training is needed, by whom, when, and where. Without identifying the need for training, there is no guarantee that the right training will be provided for the employees. Furthermore, training needs assessment may also reveal if training is the appropriate solution to a performance problem, since staff training is not the answer to all organisational problems. Other variables such as tools and equipment, job design, quality of supervision, and the existing reward systems may impact on individual performance and may not have any training implication at all.

To ensure an effective training programme, needs must be measured considering the organisation, the task itself, the individual employee and specific populations of the workforce. Therefore, there are four levels of needs analysis: *Organisational analysis, Task (or Job) analysis, Person analysis, and Demographic analysis.* The aforementioned levels of needs analysis are listed in Table 3.3, whereas the data sources for training needs analysis are presented in Table 3.4.

The design phase

After the needs assessment phase, the objectives of the training programme should be defined. Setting clear goals is vital for the effective design of a training programme since it enables human resource development profes-sionals to structure their activities with relevance and establish a basis for evaluating their efforts. An *objective* is a description of a performance which learners should be able to exhibit before they are considered com-petent. An objective should describe the result of the doing, the conditions under which the performance is to occur as well as the criteria of accept-able performance. A frequently used mnemonic for useful objectives is 'SMART'; that is, objectives must be Specific, Measurable, Achievable, Relevant (to the training activities), and Time-based. Programme object-ives need to be translated into a *lesson plan*, which is the trainer's guide

Table 3.3 Levels of training needs analysis

Levels of needs analysis	What is measured
Organisational analysis	Where is training needed and in what conditions will the training be conducted?
Task analysis	What must be done to perform the job effectively?
Person analysis	Who should be trained? What kind of training do they need?
Demographic analysis	Are there any groups within the organisation that may have different training and development needs?

Table 3.4 Data sources for training needs analysis

Sources of data for Organisational needs analysis	Implications
Organisational goals and objectives	Where human resource training emphasis can and should be placed. These provide normative standards of both direction and expected impact, which can highlight deviations from objectives and performance problems.
Human resource (manpower) inventory	Where human resource training is needed to fill gaps caused by retirement, turnover, etc.
Skills inventory	Number of employees in each skill group, knowledge and skill levels, training time per job, etc. This provides an estimate of the magnitude of the specific needs for human resource training. Useful in cost-benefit analysis of human resource training projects.
Organisational climate indexes (labour-management data such as strikes and lockouts, grievances, turnover, absenteeism, productivity, accidents, short-term sickness, observation of employee behaviour, attitude surveys, customer complaints) Analysis of efficiency indexes (costs of labour, costs of material, quality of product, equipment utilisation, costs of distribution, waste, downtime, late deliveries, repairs)	These 'quality of working life' indicators at the organisation level may help focus on problems that have human resource training components. All of these items related to either work participation or productivity are useful both in discrepancy analysis and in helping management set a value on the behaviours it wishes improved through training once human resource training has been established as a relevant solution. Cost accounting concepts may represent ratio between actual performance and desired or standard performance.
Exit interviews	Often information (i.e. problem areas) not otherwise available can be obtained in these interviews.

Sources of data for Task analysis	Implications
Job descriptions	Outlines the job in terms of typical duties and responsibilities but is not meant to be all-inclusive. Helps define performance discrepancies.
Job specifications or task analysis	List specified tasks required for each job. More specific than job descriptions. Specifications may extend to judgements of knowledge, skills, and other attributes required of job incumbents.
Performance standards	Objectives of the tasks of the job and standards by which they are judged.

Sources of data for Task analysis	*Implications*
Perform the job	Most effective way of determining specific tasks but has serious limitations (e.g. time constraints).
Review literature concerning the job (research in other industries, professional journals, documents, government sources)	Possibly useful in comparison analyses of job structures but far removed from either unique aspects of the job structure within any specific organisation or specific performance requirements.

Data sources available for Person needs assessment	*Implications*
Performance data or appraisals as indicators of problems or weaknesses (productivity, absenteeism or tardiness, accidents, short-term sickness, grievances, waste, late deliveries, product quality, downtime, repairs, equipment utilisation, customer complaints)	Include weaknesses and areas of improvement as well as strong points. Easy to analyse and quantify for purposes of determining subjects and kinds of training needed. These data can be used to identify performance discrepancies.
Observation work sampling	More subjective technique but provides both employee behaviour and results of the behaviour.
Interviews	The individual is the only one who knows what he (she) believes he (she) needs to learn. Involvement in need analysis can also motivate employees to make an effort to learn.
Questionnaires	Same approach as for the interview. Easily tailored to specific characteristics of the organisation. May produce bias through the necessity of pre-structured categories.
Tests (job knowledge, skills, achievement)	Can be tailor-made or standardised. Care must be taken so that they measure job-related qualities.
Attitude surveys	On the individual basis, useful in determining morale, motivation, or satisfaction of each employee.
Critical incidents	Observed actions that are critical to the successful or unsuccessful performance of the job.
Diaries	Individual employee records provide details of their job.
Devised situations (role play, case study, business games, in-baskets, training sessions)	Certain knowledge, skills and attitudes are demonstrated in these techniques.
Assessment centres	Combination of several of the above techniques into an intensive assessment programme.

continued

Table 3.4 Continued

Data source available for Demographic needs assessment	Implications
Human resource (manpower) inventory	Where human resource training is needed to fill gaps caused by retirement, turnover, etc. This provides also an important demographic database regarding possible scope of training needs.

for the implementation of the training session. A lesson plan involves the content to be covered in a training session, the selection of the method of instruction to be used and timing and planning of each part of the training session.

After the programme objectives have been identified, an organisation must decide whether to purchase a training and development programme from an outside source (e.g. consulting firms, educational institutions) or design it internally (in-house training) or even use some combination of the two (i.e. the organisation designs internally only a part of the training activity and purchases the remainder from an external provider). A number of factors may affect this decision, such as the size and available budget of the organisation, the number of trainees (e.g. the larger the number of trainees the greater the likelihood the organisation would be willing to design the programme itself, since it is cost efficient), the availability of time (e.g. time constraints may force an organisation to hire an outside agency to design and deliver the training programme to facilitate the process) and the expertise of the organisation (e.g. when an organisation does not have the expertise to design the programme in-house, then an outside vendor should be hired). The final steps in the design phase of the training process are the selection of the appropriate training techniques, the preparation of the relevant training material and the scheduling of the training programme (i.e. during or after work hours).

The main advantages and disadvantages of on-the-job and off-the-job training are presented in Table 3.5.

The implementation phase

The training and development methods available for the delivery of the planned training programme can be divided in three main categories: on-the-job, off-the-job, and a combination of both. On-the-job training concerns training activities conducted at a trainee's normal work setting, while off-the-job training concerns training activities conducted away from the

Table 3.5 Advantages and disadvantages of on-/off-the-job training

Advantages of on-the-job training	Disadvantages of on-the-job training
• Immediate full familiarisation with work content and environment • Learning directly linked to doing • Immediate apparentness of job development opportunities • Cost-effective method since no training facilities required	• Disruption of regular work flows and patterns • Variable cost of training instructors • Fixed costs in terms of priority and attitude shifts • Poor physical environment (noises, phone calls, etc.) which influences the learning process

Advantages of off-the-job training	Disadvantages of off-the-job training
• Ideal learning environment • Appropriate for large number of trainees • Permits the use of a variety of training techniques such as video, lecture, discussion, etc. • Costs of frustration when what has been learned cannot be put into practice	• Poor transfer of knowledge • Usually high cost (training material and facilities required)

employee's workstation. A combination of both involves training activities which may take place both at the job site and away from the workplace.

The most popular training techniques used for on-the-job training involve *Coaching and Observational learning*. 'Coaching' is a one-to-one instruction in which an employee's supervisor sets a good example of what is to be done and then examines the employee's performance and offers counselling on how to maintain effective performance and correct performance problems. This technique is discussed more extensively in Chapter 4. 'Observational learning' is a process where the employee observes a task which is done by others (e.g. supervisors, managers, co-workers) who serve as role models and the employee then performs the observed act. This is a process of learning from other people's experience by simulating their behaviour.

On the other hand, the most popular training technique available for off-the-job training includes *Classroom-based training*. This is a technique where formal teaching takes place using audiovisual and static media such as video, handouts and books. A variety of views as well as experiences can be exchanged among trainees. The emphasis in learning is usually on providing background knowledge on a specific topic. This form of training usually includes the following training tools:

- Case studies: these are 'real-life' business situations where the learners need to use their analytical and problem-solving skills to produce solutions to real or hypothetical situations. It is important for the trainer to use several probing questions and keeping everyone involved.

- Role-play: this is a highly interactive tool where the learners act out a particular role to develop a range of 'soft' skills including negotiation, and communication (see Chapter 6). It is important for the trainer to encourage a learner to take the situation seriously in order to be willing to play a role in the correct fashion.

- In-basket exercises: this is a tool where learners need to make decisions (in writing within a specific timeframe) on the letters, emails and notes typically seen on a working day. It is an activity where learners develop their ability to organise their workload and set priorities.

- Business games: this is a tool where learners need to make decisions on specific organisational problems under time and competitive pressures. Computerised formats also permit rapid feedback to the learners.

Another popular off-the-job training technique is simulation. In cases where the risks and costs involved in training on real equipment are very high, then the use of simulators (simulated experience) is suitable for employee training. Simulation is a training device designed to reproduce a work situation in a risk-controlled environment (e.g. machine simulators to train airline pilots).

A combination of on-the-job and off-the-job training involves mainly *Computer-based training*. This type of training can be done in a variety of settings and can be used as a self-paced training method as well. Computer-based training may include distance learning university courses, teaching of computer literacy skills, simulations and business games. Technological developments in IT have enabled the widespread use of computers as a learning vehicle. Extensive software developments make it possible to provide various interactive exercises and simulations. Instructional staff are used only as reference points with the emphasis being placed on self-directed learning. Web-based training refers to training that is delivered on public or private computer networks and is displayed by a web browser. Intranet-based training refers to training delivered by a company's own computer network and is restricted to a company's employees. On reviewing the advantages of e-learning, these include the flexibility of place and time, immediate feedback, and reduced training time and cost. However, e-learning based methods come with various limitations including learner isolation, motivational issues and, in several cases, low quality of help and support.

As far as the decision regarding the selection of appropriate training methods and techniques is concerned, a number of factors should be considered such as the time and money available to design and deliver an effective training programme, trainee characteristics, objectives of the training programme and availability of human and physical resources. For example, a lack of well-qualified trainers or a lack of adequate training facilities may force an organisation to choose on-the-job training techniques to deliver the training programme (e.g. coaching or mentoring) instead of using off-the-job training (e.g. simulation).

At this stage, it would be useful to outline some core principles that all trainers should follow when delivering various training interventions:

- Be well prepared to discuss their training material and should take care to ensure the provision of the right balance of information – that is, how much of one thing and how much of another is provided to the learners.
- Have a clear teaching plan or else learners will feel lost. The specific learning objectives to be achieved should be outlined at the start of the training session, whereas at the end there should be a summary of all the key learning points raised during the session.
- Be clear where the emphasis should lie. If all information is emphasised, then learners will not be able to identify the most important points.
- Follow a steady rhythm. Without due pace, communication is lifeless.
- Use various training techniques during the session to accommodate the different learning styles.
- Provide real-life examples to make the session more interesting.
- Not talk too much since the session becomes too boring (i.e. it would be useful to encourage learner interaction).
- Encourage open dialogue with the learners and avoid being autocratic.
- Seek frequent feedback from the learners regarding the learning process.

The evaluation phase

Training evaluation is the process which attempts to measure how well a training activity met its objectives. However, many organisations ignore this critical stage due to misconceptions, such as the perception that training evaluation adds cost to the training process without offering specific results about the training activity that can be transformed into specific indicators for future action. However, this is a stage that cannot be ignored since it determines the success of a training intervention and provides valuable information on areas for improvement. The most popular model of training evaluation is the four-level framework developed by Donald Kirkpatrick. To measure the effectiveness of training, Kirkpatrick (1983) suggests the following four criteria:

1   *Reactions.* This criterion evaluates the trainee's perceptions about the training programme (e.g. if they liked its content, the trainer and the methods used). Normally, structured questionnaires are used to measure this dimension.

2   *Learning.* This is a criterion which measures the extent to which learners met the training objectives of the programme. It involves special tests that give an indication of how well employees have learned particular skills.

3   *Behaviour.* This criterion examines the transfer of learning at work. It usually involves direct observation of the trainee's behaviour at work by the immediate supervisor.

4   *Results.* This criterion measures the degree to which the training intervention improved the organisation's effectiveness. It involves a cost-benefit analysis by providing data and information on productivity, sales, absenteeism, staff turnover rate, and error rate before and after training, etc.

A detailed list of the available sources for training evaluation is presented in Table 3.6.

Facilitating learning transfer from off-the-job training interventions

Learning transfer is the process through which organisations promote a climate where employees can positively transfer newly acquired skills to the job. In short, this involves the application of skills to the workplace. The core principles of learning transfer are outlined below:

•   Transfer is a function of a system of influences – not just learning design. Transfer can only be completely understood and influenced by examining the entire system of influences. The variables affecting learning transfer are: trainer variables (e.g. competence), organisational factors (e.g. job design and reward systems), content and delivery of the training programme, trainee characteristics (e.g. ability, motivation) and so on.

•   Achieving transfer does not require substantial new processes and systems. The challenge is not how to build a bigger and more influential

Table 3.6 Sources of training evaluation

Evaluation data collection methods	Advantages	Disadvantages
Interview	• Flexible • Opportunity for clarification • Depth possible	• High cost • Time-consuming • Trained observers needed
Questionnaire	• Low cost • Anonymity possible • Variety of options	• Possible inaccurate data return rate beyond control
Written Test	• Low purchase cost • Easily administered • Quickly processed • Wide sampling possible	• Possible low relation to job performance
Direct Observation	• Excellent way to measure behaviour change	• May be unreliable • Trained observers needed • Possibly disruptive
Archival Performance data	• Objective • Reliable • Job-based	• May be expensive to collect • Information system discrepancies

support system; it is, rather, how to make transfer a more integral part of the existing organisational climate.

• Transfer interventions will be most successful where the explicit goal is performance improvement. Learning activities have often been created more as a reward than as a way to truly improve work performance. If managers are to truly understand and build interventions that will improve learning transfer, then it is important that they do so when performance really matters to the learning sponsors.

• The organisation should be structured for optimal learning transfer. This involves creating practices that enable employees to apply learning at work such as, job design considerations, IT systems to capture knowledge, proper rewards for the application of new skills at work, managerial coaching, and goal-setting that encourages the use of new skills.

4   Informal learning at work

Informal learning defined

Technological developments, the rise of the global economy and the emergence of 'knowledge work' have resulted not only in unprecedented demands for learning and knowledge, but also in a shift away from the view in which planned training interventions were regarded as the principal locus of learning, towards a perspective in which informal (unplanned) learning experiences at work are increasingly acknowledged as an important source of skills development. *Informal learning* is that which results from daily life activities relating to work, the domestic arena or leisure. It is sometimes referred to as experiential learning and can to some extent be understood as learning that is accidental.

Several writers have argued that there are two forms of knowledge within the workplace: explicit knowledge, which is codified and formally transmitted between employees and within organisations; and tacit knowledge, which is not codified, but is instead deeply ingrained in the practices of particular social and cultural contexts within organisations. The significance of tacit knowledge within the workplace, and the potential for this to positively influence workplace performance, is well recognised by the academic community but poorly understood. In line with the growing interest in informal learning, increasing attention is now being focused on developing an understanding of how tacit knowledge can be converted into explicit knowledge, so that that which is hidden may be released and utilised for the benefit of organisations. In this context, several academics have pointed out that tacit knowledge has to be learned implicitly, and within the context of the workplace this suggestion implies a significant role for learning that is informal and on-the-job.

Benefits and limitations of informal learning

It has been suggested in the literature that formal off–the-job learning is most appropriate in developing specific skills in organisations where roles are clearly specified and circumscribed, and where each employee occupies a position within a clearly defined hierarchy of authority. This approach has, however, been increasingly challenged by organisational restructuring, and by the trend towards flatter organisations in which authority is devolved and the responsibilities of employees broadened. Such developments have necessitated the development of new skills, especially in areas such as problem-solving and team-working, which cannot be readily acquired from the discontinuous learning episodes characteristic of the formal off-the-job training course. Furthermore, there is also the problem of training transfer. Informal, on-the-job learning enables such issues to be addressed, and also takes place at the appropriate time, i.e. at the actual point where employees need to apply new skills and knowledge rather than before this, which affects the learning transfer process. Against this backdrop there is now a substantial research base suggesting that informal on-the-job learning is the most significant route by which employees acquire and develop the skills and competences required for effective performance within the workplace.

Informal learning is particularly important within the small business sector due to various resource constraints that such organisations face resulting in employees being much less likely than those in larger ones to have the opportunity to participate in off-the-job learning interventions. Furthermore, informal learning is especially valuable for small enterprises because they occupy increasingly specialist markets and thus have a need for high-specificity skills rather than generic skills (mostly developed through formal training). However, it should be noted that an over-reliance on informal learning may limit the scope that employees have for learning through reflection. Formal learning is a necessary building block, providing employees with the theoretical knowledge and conceptual tools that enable them to work effectively in environments that are increasingly demanding intellectual capacity, as well as the confidence to cross disciplinary and skill boundaries. Informal learning has less capacity to deliver the conceptual and theoretical understanding that facilitates such behaviours.

Evaluating the effectiveness of informal learning

As much on-the-job learning is informal in character it is by its very nature unplanned and ad hoc. Such learning is therefore not amenable to the traditional approaches utilised to measure formal learning, since learning outcomes cannot be specified. Specifying and measuring the learning outcomes generated by unplanned learning is highly problematic, since indicators traditionally used in the field of education and training, such as participation rates, training hours, expenditures or level of qualification achieved are inappropriate in this context, as they relate primarily to the inputs and outcomes of formal learning. It should become clear that on-the-job learning is unplanned, so it is difficult to detect without prolonged observation. This is especially the case because employees engaged in on-the-job learning have a tendency to regard this as a normal part of everyday work, and do not interpret their actions within the framework of learning. Perhaps because of these difficulties, few academic studies have examined the effectiveness of on-the-job learning specifically, and little hard data exists in relation to how this supports workplace development and performance outcomes. Yet the few academic studies that have considered the impact of informal learning have found a positive relationship between this and employee or organisational performance.

Main forms of informal learning

Guided learning

Learning in the workplace is the product of everyday thinking and acting. Rather than being an activity that is switched on or off, therefore, learning is a continuous activity. The available literature suggests that guidance within the workplace is likely to increase the robustness of learning, but differentiates between two forms of this. First, *direct guidance* is manifest in experts guiding novices' choice of solutions to tasks, providing models, clues and cues to appropriate performance and facilitating staged access to increasingly demanding activities (coaching). Second, *indirect guidance*, by contrast, is premised upon novices observing and listening to their colleagues (observational learning).

The strengths of guided on-the-job learning are that it structures workplace experiences, thus enabling the novice to move to activities that are increasingly accountable at a comfortable pace. Direct guidance also militates against the development of inappropriate knowledge that might give rise to unsuitable workplace practices and behaviours. However, a weakness of the guided learning approach is that experts or co-workers may be unwilling to share their knowledge and expertise with novices, particularly if they are concerned about the possibility of being replaced by those whom they have guided and supported. An unwillingness to share knowledge may also be evident if experts interpret the diffusion of knowledge in terms of loss of status, or regard knowledge-sharing to be against their interests.

Tips for effective coaching

- *Keep a steady pace of guidance.*
- *Try to accommodate different learning styles.*
  As mentioned in Chapter 1, every individual learns differently. Technically, an individual's learning style refers to the preferential way in which the person absorbs processes and comprehends and retains information. For example, when learning how to sell a product effectively, some employees understand the process by following verbal instructions, while others have to see it in practice. Individual learning styles depend on cognitive, emotional and environmental factors, as well as one's prior experience. It is therefore important for a manager to understand the differences in their employees' learning styles, so that they can implement best-practice strategies into their daily activities when coaching.
- *Provide constructive feedback*
  Feedback that is constructive is vital to employees' ongoing development. Feedback clarifies expectations, helps people learn from their mistakes and builds confidence. Feedback is best given shortly after managers have observed a specific type of behaviour. Moreover, feedback should be clear and specific. For instance, you may explain to your employee the impact their behaviour had on team performance and provide clear suggestions as to how the employee could do things differently. Avoid using negative comments that discourage your employees, such as, 'You shouldn't talk to the customer in this way....' This may affect employee morale in a negative way. Always try to be encouraging and use comments that start with: 'Maybe you could try talking to the customer in this way ...', or 'Have you considered doing ...?' It has to be clear from the start that you are providing this feedback to help your employees improve their performance – not to embarrass them. In short, try to use positive language in order to develop your staff.
- *Use Effective communication*
  - Use descriptive not evaluative statements.
  - Use problem-oriented statements rather than person-oriented.
  - Use equality-oriented statements by giving the message that the recipient is valued and worthwhile and that you want the interaction to be mutually satisfying.
  - Use statements that acknowledge the other's person importance and uniqueness.

- Use empathy in listening to the statements of others by paying attention to the content of the message, the feelings behind the message and any implicit meaning that may underlie the message.
- Be sensitive to signs of resistance.
- Use a variety of responses to others' statements depending on the goal of the communication and the strength of the relationship.
- Have a positive approach even in difficult situations, an important element of coaching.
- Listen and encourage.
- Generate responsibility and ownership.
- Build trust by developing a real relationship.
- Set specific goals to be achieved.

Action learning

Action learning is an approach to learning that is based on individuals working on real problems that have the capacity to be solved by action. It therefore involves individuals identifying a problem, taking ownership of it, and identifying the steps necessary to resolve it. These processes involve a group of co-workers who learn primarily by questioning their own and others' proposed actions in relation to the problem that has been identified. In this way, they learn new skills and develop broader insights. However, the effectiveness of action learning is to some extent dependent upon learners being able to identify and address their own learning needs within this process. In practical terms this may indicate that action learning needs a facilitator who understands it as a process, and is able to initiate and promote this approach. A further difficulty associated with action learning within the workplace is that because the outcomes are dependent upon change, the action learning process may be perceived as a threat, and may be met with resistance from those who have a vested interest in preserving the status quo.

Communities of practice

This concept actually stands in contrast to the traditional educational perspectives in which the learner (or, within the workplace, the employee) is regarded as the passive recipient of taught knowledge. This is a form of learning which supports learning occurring in context, and that new entrants to the workplace therefore gain knowledge and skills through a process of 'legitimate peripheral participation'. This process involves new employees progressively engaging with workplace activities so that over time from being marginal members of the work group they emerge as full participants within an established 'community of practice'. In other words, employees develop skills on-the-job through engaging in tasks and with colleagues, but as the meaning of this activity is defined and negotiated by the work group novices are also able to access the hidden curriculum of the workplace. In this sense new employees engage in peripheral participation in order to 'catch up' with experienced employees, yet the process of peripheral participation commonly occurs naturally within the workplace and is often beyond the control and capture of management.

However, it should be acknowledged that communities of practice are social structures involving power relations, and that the way in which power is exercised can influence learning outcomes. This means that peripheral members of a community of practice may not necessarily achieve full membership status as a result of power imbalances within such structures, and that their learning may be restricted as a consequence. In short, trust, familiarity and mutual understanding are prerequisites for the successful transfer of tacit knowledge, and members of communities of practice may be less willing to share knowledge and expertise in situations where trust is lacking or compromised.

Job rotation

Job rotation is a process that involves transfers of employees between jobs within an organisation. Many early commentators advocated job rotation as a mechanism to increase employee motivation, because this approach relieved the boredom and fatigue experienced by those engaged in the highly standardised and repetitive jobs characteristic of the mass production paradigm. However, job rotation is also an effective way of developing employee competence, since this facilitates on-the-job learning. Intra-functional rotation within higher levels of organisational hierarchies, for instance, enables employees to gain a deeper understanding of their organisations, and is therefore especially useful in succession planning. Yet intra-functional rotation at lower levels within organisational hierarchies enables employees to learn how to perform a broader range of tasks and functions and thus supports flexible working. Although job rotation offers some scope to enable employees to improve their existing skills, clearly the capacity for organisations to utilise this methodology will depend to a large extent on the nature of their business and the types of jobs that employees do.

Factors affecting informal learning

Competitive strategy

According to several research studies, skill formation and workplace learning are, in strategic management terms, normally third-order issues in most organisations. First-order questions relate to competitive strategy. They impact upon second-order choices, which concern, among other things, the nature of the work organisation, job design and performance management systems. Decisions about workplace learning rest within the wider contexts provided by first- and second-order decision-making; hence it may be necessary to encourage employers to change their competitive strategies in order to change their approach to learning within the workplace. If employers seek to upgrade product market strategies and enhance product specification and service quality they will maximise the opportunities for the entire workforce to engage in learning in order to acquire and utilise higher levels of skill. In short, training resources may be wasted within companies operating on the basis of low-value-added products using a system of mass production unless those organisations have a business strategy that locates skill as the primary source of competitive advantage. Although there is evidence to indicate that even organisations following the 'high-quality' road may create jobs that trap employees into routine, low-skilled jobs, it has been shown that employee learning is regarded as a key mechanism to assist staff to adapt to the changes needed to enable organisations to follow this pathway.

Organisational structure

The structure of an organisation can also exert a significant influence on learning and skills development within the workplace. Organisational structures that encourage team-working and collaboration are able to stimulate demand for informal on-the-job learning, whereas hierarchical structures, and those that do not provide employees with the opportunity to cooperate and work collectively, can act as barriers to this.

Organisational culture

Many commentators have further highlighted the significance of organisational culture to the opportunities that employees have to engage in, in on-the-job learning. Indeed, a learning culture within organisations, that is, a culture in which workplace learning is promoted, supported and rewarded, is a major facilitator of informal on-the-job learning. In all organisations a psychological contract exists between the employer and employee. This sets expected standards for work activity and performance and anticipated support among employees. If there is a perceived discrepancy between espoused company policy and actual practice, employees may be unwilling to develop new skills.

The organisation of work

The way in which work is organised has been identified by many writers as a major influence on the opportunities that employees have for on-the-job learning. Forms of work organisation that are premised upon cooperation and collaboration between employees have significantly more potential to promote on-the-job learning than forms of work organisation that are based upon employees working in isolation. Moreover, a close and dependent relationship with a supervisor also appears to facilitate on-the-job learning. Organisations that choose to organise work in such a way that the majority of employees undertake a relatively narrow range of tasks, with limited job autonomy and little real involvement in work, will end up offering very few opportunities for on-the-job learning. The shift towards a high-skills workplace that would facilitate on-the-job learning, therefore, would necessitate the introduction of forms of work organisation in which employees have a greater degree of control over the labour process.

Job design

The opportunities that employees have to learn at work are greatly influenced by the nature and content of the jobs they do, the way that the jobs are structured and controlled, and the responsibilities that are given to or withheld from those undertaking them. The opportunities for development within work will affect the opportunities employees have for on-the-job learning, and thus the skills they can develop. Challenging work provides more opportunities than does work of a routine nature for employees to learn on the job, as well as to apply any newly acquired skills.

The role of managers

The role of managers as gatekeepers to formal learning opportunities within the workplace has long been recognised, but their role in relation to promoting a learning culture, and facilitating informal on-the-job learning, has received increasing attention in recent years. Supervisors and managers can provide assistance to those for whom they have responsibility as they learn on-the-job, are able to provide a model of behaviours that on-the-job learning aims to develop and can offer positive feedback on the use of skills developed through on-the-job learning approaches.

Performance management frameworks and reward systems

Performance reviews and appraisal schemes are considered to be particularly important since these enable employees to clarify their performance objectives, and, perhaps more importantly, identify the skills they need to develop in order to facilitate this. The provision of rewards for knowledge-sharing, teamwork and on-the-job learning also has the potential to promote such activity. Performance management frameworks need both to complement, rather than impede, workplace learning, and to ensure that managers play a key role in facilitating this. In short, on-the-job learning could be promoted by rewards in the shape of positive feedback from supervisors, higher wages for increased proficiency or competence, access to more interesting tasks, or enhanced career opportunities.

The role of trade unions

A number of writers have highlighted the positive contribution that trade unions are able to make to workplace learning. More specifically, it has been suggested that if trade unions are able to close off routes to competitiveness based on low skills and low wages, this is likely to encourage employers to adopt alternative high-skills, high-wage strategies, and by implication, to invest in learning that will improve the skill levels of employees.

Individual factors

A number of individual factors should not be ignored when talking about the factors affecting informal learning. These include employee motivation, individual aspirations and prior experiences of learning. For example, if employees do not have the desire to share their knowledge with their peers for various reasons, then the process of informal learning will not be supported. Similarly, if employees are not motivated to expand their skills (e.g. owing to poor career development opportunities within a firm), then they will not participate actively in various informal learning opportunities.

5   Creating the learning organisation

Types of organisational learning

The salient feature of an organisation is that it is a matter of people cooperating: thinking things out together, taking decisions and carrying out activities. Collective learning is aimed at increasing the collective competence of the members of an organisation and it is essentially equivalent to organisational change. In the following paragraphs, an analysis is conducted on how organisational learning takes place.

Single loop learning: This is the process of collective learning that brings about changes in the existing rules. It involves learning at the rules level. For example, a vocational institution of post-secondary education suffers from a radical decline in applications from new students. It is decided by the senior management team to intensify publicity of the available educational programmes by creating a new prospectus and attending various educational fairs.

Double loop learning: This is the process of collective learning that brings about changes in the underlying insights. It involves learning at the level of insight. For example, the vocational institution of post-secondary education mentioned above starts wondering about the curriculum it offers and the overall learning atmosphere within the college.

Triple loop learning: This is the process where the essential principles on which the organisation is founded come into discussion. It refers to the position of the organisation in the market, the role it aims to fulfil and the identity it has. In the above example of the educational institution, this would concern the decision to transform radically the educational programmes offered by the institution.

The learning organisation: main characteristics

In simple words, a learning organisation is one that facilitates the learning of all its members and continuously transforms itself to achieve superior competitive performance. The concept of the learning organisation encompasses learning both at the individual level (e.g. knowledge and skills acquisition) and the organisational level (e.g. team learning). In this context, the human resource training and development activity is a vital part of the learning organisation since it constitutes a basic element of individual learning. The underlying philosophy of the learning organisation is to enhance the achievement of collective goals by harnessing the reservoir of knowledge, skills and insights of all the members of the organisation.

A number of authors have developed models of the learning-conducive workplace environment. Many studies suggest that the workplace environment influences employee learning on three distinct levels: organisational, functional and personal. Within this framework, the availability of Human Resource Development capacity in the form of the facilitation of skills, learning expertise and the capacity to develop flexible solutions to learning needs, as well as financial resources, is key to the creation of a learning conducive environment, alongside management support for learning and employee willingness to engage in learning activities.

According to the findings of several studies on the learning organisation, the creation of expansive learning environments would enable employees to participate in multiple communities of practice both within and beyond the workplace. First, they would enable employees to engage in learning by participation in cross-company activities. Second, they would support learning across the whole workforce and would have a multi-dimensional conceptualisation of expertise. Third, they would value teamwork and, finally, they would regard managers as facilitators of learning and would provide opportunities for employees to learn new skills and jobs. A restrictive learning environment, by contrast, would limit the capacity of employees to participate in multiple communities of practice both within and beyond the workplace and their opportunities to engage in learning by participation in cross-company activities; would emphasise job-specific learning; would support learning among selected members of the workforce and would have a uni-dimensional, top-down conceptualisation of expertise; would value rigid specialist roles; would regard managers as controllers of the workforce; and would provide limited opportunities for employees to learn new skills and jobs.

Other influential theoretical models of learning-conducive environments relate solely to informal learning. Such models indicate that informal learning is more likely to occur among employees that are engaged in roles that are characterised by:

• A high degree of change in terms of products or processes, technology or work organisation;

- A high level of demands in terms of customer expectation, suppliers, owners and/or professional communities requiring exacting standards;
- Having access to learning resources such as advice and guidance from colleagues, access to databases, literature etc., and the time to utilise such resources;
- Some level of managerial responsibility for decision-making, project management, work group management, etc;
- Opportunities to engage with networks beyond the immediate working environment by, for example participating in professional forums;
- Feedback on learning through work;
- Managerial support and encouragement for learning in the workplace;
- Human resource policies that reward proficiency.

Organisations with transparent boundaries that expose more employees to the external environment, that have flatter hierarchies in which managerial responsibilities are more evenly distributed and which have high levels of employee involvement in product and process development would be most conducive to informal on-the-job learning. To sum up, learning organisations display a number of characteristics. They thus:

- Create new knowledge as a central part of competitive strategy
- Capitalise on uncertainty as a source of growth
- Embrace change
- Encourage accountability at the lowest levels
- Encourage managers to act as mentors, coaches and learning facilitators
- Have a culture of feedback and disclosure
- Have a holistic systemic view of organisational systems, processes and relationships
- Have a shared, organisation-wide vision, purpose and values
- Have leaders who encourage risk taking and experimentation
- Have systems for sharing knowledge and using it in the business
- Are customer driven
- Are involved in the broader community
- Link employee development and organisational development
- Network within the business community
- Provide frequent opportunities for experiential learning
- Avoid bureaucracy
- Have a high trust culture
- Strive for continuous improvement
- Structure, foster and reward all types of teamwork
- Use cross-functional work teams
- View the unexpected as an opportunity to learn.

6   Development of 'soft' skills

Definition and importance of 'soft' skills

Although much has been written about how to develop the 'hard' skills of workers, much less is known about the genesis of 'soft' skills. However, understanding the obstacles to developing soft skills and then addressing them is crucial for the workplace since soft skills do make the difference in employee performance as they constitute all those personal qualities that employees need in order to interact effectively with others at work and complete their tasks. The list of soft skills is extensive and includes communication, team-working, empathy, self-awareness, conflict management, problem-solving, negotiation, adaptability and motivation.

Most employees have learned not to trust their emotions. They have been told emotions distort the more accurate information our intellect supplies. On the other hand, our abilities to memorise and problem-solve, to spell words and to do mathematical calculations, are easily measured on written tests. Ultimately, these intellectual abilities dictate which career paths individuals are advised to follow. However, intelligence quotient (IQ) is usually less important in determining how successful individuals are than emotional quotient (EQ), which is the ability to identify, use, understand and manage our emotions in positive and constructive ways. It is well known that there are people who are academically brilliant and yet are socially inept and unsuccessful. What they are missing is emotional intelligence. There is a world of difference between knowledge and behaviour, or applying that knowledge to make changes in our lives. There are many things people may know and want to do, but do not or cannot when they are under pressure. This is especially true when it comes to emotional intelligence.

Emotional intelligence is not learned in the standard intellectual way; it must be learned and understood on an emotional level. People cannot simply read about emotional intelligence or master it through memorisation. In order to learn about emotional intelligence in a way that produces change, people need to engage the emotional parts of the brain in ways that connect them to others. This kind of learning is based on what people see, hear and feel. Intellectual understanding is an important first step, but the development of emotional intelligence depends on *sensory, non-verbal learning* and *real-life practice*. In the following paragraphs, detailed guidance is provided to HR and line managers on how to develop a number of core employee 'soft' skills.

Skill 1: the ability to quickly reduce stress

There is already a bulk of research indicating that an excessive amount of stress overwhelms the mind and body, thus affecting individual ability to accurately understand a situation, be aware of one's own feelings and needs, and communicate clearly. Therefore, one of the core 'soft' skills that employees should develop is the ability to quickly calm themselves down when they are feeling overwhelmed. Being able to manage stress in the moment is the key to resilience. This skill helps employees to stay balanced, focused and in control regardless of the challenges they might face.

Steps to help your employees reduce their stress are as follows:

- *Guide them towards realising when they are stressed*: The first step to reducing stress is recognising what stress feels like (the physiological and psychological symptoms).
- *Help them to identify their stress response*: Everyone reacts differently to stress. The best way to quickly calm themselves depends on their specific stress response.
- *Guide them towards discovering the stress reduction techniques that work for them*: There are several techniques to reduce stress in a quick manner, including: meditation; exercise; talking to others in order to externalise the problem and seek help, as well as find new ways to tackle problems; and behaviour control (i.e. recognising and changing your behaviour patterns). As a trainer, you can teach employees to practise the ABC technique in order to change their thinking patterns (i.e. turn negative thoughts into positives). The acronym ABC stands for: *Adversity* (i.e. the activating event that might cause intense stress); *Belief* (i.e. how individuals perceive/explain the event); and *Consequence* (i.e. the behavioural impact of thinking patterns). The stress situation occurs between the activating event and the belief. So, it is important to identify the 'problematic' beliefs and change them. There are three major dimensions to people's explanatory style:

permanence (i.e. bad events are permanent); pervasiveness (universal statement about your life); and personalisation (internalise blame). As a trainer, you should work on these areas with the learners.

Skill 2: the ability to recognise and manage emotions

The second key soft skill is an individual's ability to understand their emotions and how they influence their thoughts and actions. Emotional self-awareness is the key to understanding yourself and others. Many individuals are disconnected from their core emotions such as anger, sadness, fear and joy. But although we can distort, deny or numb our feelings, we cannot eliminate them. They remain there, whether we are aware of them or not. Unfortunately, without emotional awareness, individuals are unable to fully understand their own needs or to communicate effectively with others.

In order to be emotionally healthy and emotionally intelligent, people must reconnect to their core emotions, accept them and become comfortable with them. If employees are self-aware, they always know how they feel. And they know how their emotions and their actions can affect the people around them. Being self-aware means having a clear picture of their strengths and weaknesses.

Steps to help your employees improve their self-awareness:

* *Encourage them to keep a journal*: Journals help improve their self-awareness. If they could spend just a few minutes each day writing down their thoughts and feelings this can move them to a higher degree of self-awareness (e.g. what was my though about this event? How did I feel? Why?).
* *Urge them to slow down*: When they experience any strong emotions, they should be able to slow down to examine why. Remind them of the fact that no matter what the situation, they can always *choose* how they react to it.

Self-regulation is closely linked to self-awareness since it is about staying in control. Employees who regulate themselves effectively rarely verbally attack others, make poor decisions, stereotype people, or compromise their values.

Steps to help your employees improve their self-regulation:

* *Guide them to identify carefully their values*: Do they know what values are most important to them? Encourage them to spend some time examining their 'code of ethics'.

• *Help them to admit their mistakes*: If your employees tend to blame others when something goes wrong, make them reflect on that. Encourage them to admit to their mistakes and face the consequences, whatever they are.

• *Help them to achieve a state of calmness*: have your employees practise deep-breathing exercises to calm themselves. Also, urge them to write down on a piece of paper all of the negative things they want to say, and let them throw it away. Expressing these emotions on paper is better than speaking them aloud to their colleagues.

Skill 3: the ability to connect with others using non-verbal communication

Being a good communicator requires more than just verbal skills. More often than not, *what* we say is less important than *how* we say it or the other non-verbal signals we send out. In order to hold the attention of others and build connection and trust, we need to be aware of and in control of our non-verbal cues. We also need to be able to accurately read and respond to the non-verbal cues that other people send us. Non-verbal communication is also a core soft skill. This wordless form of communication is emotionally driven. It is about the way we listen, look, move, and react. Our non-verbal messages will produce a sense of interest, trust, excitement, and desire for connection – or they will generate fear, confusion, distrust, and disinterest. Part of improving non-verbal communication involves paying attention to: eye contact; facial expression; tone of voice; posture and gesture; touch; timing and pace.

Skill 4: the ability to resolve conflicts positively and with confidence

Conflict and disagreements are inevitable in relationships. Two people cannot possibly have the same needs, opinions, and expectations at all times. However, resolving conflict in healthy, constructive ways can strengthen trust between people. When conflict is not perceived as threatening or punishing, it fosters freedom, creativity, and safety in relationships. The ability to manage conflicts in a positive, trust-building way is another critical soft skill.

Steps to help your employees resolve conflicts in a trust-building way:

• *Advise them to stay focused in the present*: When we are not holding on to old resentments, we can recognise the reality of a current situation and view it as a new opportunity for resolving old feelings about conflicts.

• *Help them to choose proper arguments*: Arguments take time and energy, especially if you want to resolve them in a positive way. Urge your employees to consider what is worth arguing about and what is not.

• *Advise them to forgive*: If they continue to be hurt or mistreated, they should protect themselves. They need to keep in mind that someone else's hurtful behaviour is in the past. They need to remember that conflict-resolution involves giving up the urge to punish.

• *Advise them to adopt a suitable style of conflict-handling according to the situation*: There are various styles of conflict-handling, including: competing (solving the conflict using formal authority or/and power); compromising (partial satisfaction of both parties); collaborating (the concerns of both sides are satisfied); accommodating (yielding to another's wishes); and avoiding (you simply avoid the situation). Each style is suitable in certain situations. For example, the competing style seems to be appropriate when quick, decisive action is vital during emergencies.

Skill 5: the ability to be self-motivated

Self-motivated employees consistently work towards their goals. And they usually have extremely high standards for the quality of their work. In order to help your employees improve their motivation, three key steps should be followed:

• *Help them to re-examine why they are doing this particular job*: It is easy for them to forget what they really like about their career. So, advise them to take some time to remember why they wanted this job. If they are unhappy in their role and they are struggling to remember why they wanted it, they should try to find the root of the problem. Starting at the root often helps them look at their situation in a new way.

• *Advise them to develop goal statements that are fresh and energising.*

• *Urge them to be hopeful and find something positive*: Motivated employees are usually optimistic, no matter what they face. Adopting this mindset might take practice, but it is well worth the effort. Advise your employees every time they face a challenge, or even a failure, to find at least one good thing about the situation. It might be something small, like a new contact, or something with long-term effects, like an important lesson learned. But there is almost always something positive – they just have to look for it.

Skill 6: the ability to understand others (having empathy)

For any employee, having empathy is critical to co-operating successfully with other team members. People with empathy have the ability to put themselves in someone else's situation. They help develop the people on their team, challenge others who are acting unfairly, give constructive feedback, and listen to those who need it. The most important step to help your employees develop empathy is to teach them the 'perceptual positions', dealt with in the following section.

Different perspectives

Often, it is useful to assess an event or outcome from several different perspectives: From our own perspective, from the perspective of another person and from the perspective of an independent observer. Perceptual positions provide a balanced approach to thinking about an event or outcome. In situations where there is little or no understanding or progress, they can provide a way of developing new understandings and creating new choices.

The three perceptual positions are as follows:

*   *First Position*: seeing, hearing and feeling the situation through your own eyes, ears and feelings. You think in terms of what is important to you, what you want to achieve.
*   *Second Position*: stepping into the shoes of the other person and experiencing (seeing, hearing and feeling) the situation as if you were them. You think in terms of how this situation would appear or be interpreted by the other person.
*   *Third Position*: standing back from a situation and experiencing it as if you were a detached observer. In your mind, you are able to see and hear yourself and the other person, as if you were a third person. You think in terms of what opinion, observations or advice someone would offer who is not involved. You need to be in a strong, resourceful state and take an objective view of your own behaviour and look for opportunities to respond differently in order to achieve a different and more positive outcome.

However, sometimes people get stuck in one of the above-described positions:

*   Someone who lives his/her life in first position would tend to focus on his/her needs rather than the needs of others – a 'self-centered' attitude. It can be argued that addicts tend to see the world from first position.

- Someone who lives their life primarily in second position is always thinking about the other person at the expense of their own needs. Co-dependents would fit this description.
- Someone who lives in third position would be seen as rather aloof and a disinterested observer of life – always on the outside looking in.

All three positions are of equal importance and it is useful to encourage your employees to consciously go through these positions in order to understand other's people behaviour as they go about their daily activities. Furthermore, another important area in attempting to help your employees develop empathy is to train them to pay attention to body language. Body language tells others how people really feel about a situation. Learning to read body language can be a real asset for employees because they will be better able to determine how someone truly feels. This, in turn, gives them the opportunity to respond appropriately by addressing the other person's feelings.

Skill 7: training your employees to become creative problem-solvers

Problem-solving is a skill that is required of every employee in almost every professional context. Most employees usually face the need to solve some kinds of problems rather frequently. The job of the manager is by its very nature a problem-solving job. Therefore, it is vital for managers to help their employees develop their problem-solving skills.

Steps in problem-solving

The most popular model of problem-solving involves four major steps, which are presented in Table 6.1.

Table 6.1 Steps in problem-solving

Steps in problem-solving	Characteristics
Define the problem	State the problem explicitly. Differentiate facts from opinion.
Generate alternative solutions	Specify short-term and long-term alternatives that are consistent with goals (i.e. solve the problem).
Evaluate and select alternative	Evaluate pros and cons of each alternative. Evaluate relative to an optimal standard. State the selected alternative explicitly.
Implement and follow up on the solution	Implement at the right time and in the right sequence. Provide opportunities for feedback. Establish an ongoing monitoring system and evaluate based on problem solution.

Conceptual blocks in problem-solving

The four steps mentioned above do not always lead to the desired outcome because conceptual blocks diminish the effectiveness of problem definition. Conceptual blocks are mental obstacles that constrain the way in which the problem is defined and the number of alternative solutions considered to be relevant. The most important conceptual blocks identified in the literature are summarised in Table 6.2.

Overcoming conceptual blocks

Below are listed specific behavioural action guidelines to help your employees eliminate conceptual blocks:

- When defining a problem, try to generate at least two alternative hypotheses for every problem definition. Creative people who actively formulate antithetical ideas and then resolve them produce the most valuable contributions.
- When generating potential problem solutions, try to defer evaluating any until all have been proposed.
- Beware of your stereotypes based on past experience in dealing with problems.
- Encourage wild ideas and do not hesitate to build on others' ideas.
- Increase the number of possible solutions by combining unrelated problem attributes.

Table 6.2 Conceptual blocks that inhibit effective problem-solving

---

Focusing on a single problem definition without considering other possible definitions (i.e. vertical thinking)

Considering present problems only as variations on problems faced in the past (i.e. stereotyping)

Defining the boundaries of problems too narrowly

Failing to see relationships between different elements of the problem

Fearing to appear ignorant if questions are asked

Bias against thinking. Most people use the left hemisphere of the brain to solve a problem (this part of the brain is concerned with logical and analytical thinking; and thinking tends to be organised and precise). However, right-hemisphere thinking is concerned with synthesis and qualitative judgement and is mainly imaginative and emotional. Creative ideas arise most frequently in the right-brain hemisphere.

---

7 Giving effective presentations

Steps for improving the quality of your presentation

The quality of a presentation is generally attributed to the skills and knowledge of the presenter. More often than not, HR and other line managers will need to deliver a formal presentation as part of a training intervention. It is therefore important for them to follow some key guidelines to improve the quality of their presentation. These guidelines are discussed below.

Use physical space and movement to your advantage

Prior to your presentation, arrange the physical space and seating in the room so that distractions can be avoided. If you are speaking in a large room, arrange the audience so that they are not disturbed by late arrivals. Position yourself to enhance your rapport with the audience and try to group learners so there is little space between them. Also, try to position yourself roughly at the front, mid-point of your audience in order to maintain eye contact during your presentation.

Use gestures naturally

Physical movement can be used to stress important points, signal a transition in your presentation, build rapport with a learner asking a question, and stimulate the interest of isolated segments of the audience. Gestures should appear spontaneous and natural so that they enhance rather than distract from your message. Focus on your message, not your movements. Use a variety of gestures and avoid repeating the same over and over. Gestures can be used to describe, add emphasis and direct attention. They can also involve the entire upper body – not just your dominant hand. Be sensitive to the appearance and length of a gesture. Gestures need to be of appropriate duration just as visual aids need to be of sufficent length for comprehension purposes.

Convince the audience that you are concerned about them as learners

Prior to your presentation, learn as much as you can about the background of your audience. This will help your presentation significantly (content, emphasis, etc.). Once you begin your presentation, speak directly to individuals by maintaining eye contact with all members of the audience. Pace your delivery to the audience by watching their responses. If facial or other expressions indicate that an idea is not getting across to the audience, try to slow down. When in doubt, ask a question to confirm you have been understood. State the purpose and importance of your presentation during your introduction and conclusion. Personalise your message by demonstrating you understand the audience's fears, needs and desires. Speaking from the audience's point of view requires using their language (e.g. when you support the introduction of a new product line, you need to emphasise different points to the head of production, the president, etc.). People are more likely to listen to someone who agrees with them. It is always good to find some areas of agreement with which to begin your presentation. It is equally important to begin with the familiar. If you are presenting difficult material, try to place it in a context with which your audience feels comfortable (e.g. refer to a long-lasting organisational problem or common experience).

Present a logically compelling argument for your proposal/idea

Showing how a proposal will help the audience fulfil a common objective can substantially increase audience support. In developing a logical argument, it is important to avoid the following:

* Hasty generalisations (jumping early to conclusions)
* An interconnection of unrelated events (no relationship or insufficient relationship)
* False assumptions (e.g. we all know that a recession is inevitable, so let's begin planning for inevitable layoffs)
* Offering just two solutions when other alternatives are possible.

Hold your audience's attention by being vigorous and providing variety

Most presentations are not intense enough and end up being very boring for the learners. If you are alive, alert, focused and enthusiastic, your audience will be compelled to listen. Your posture, tone of voice and facial expressions are critical indicators of your attitude. Use novelty in your presentation. Use chalkboard, audiovisual material, demonstrations and audience participation so the use of no single approach occupies too long a period. Variety is particularly critical during lengthy presentations. Humour is also an effective source of variety and relief. However, avoid getting a laugh at the expense of the mistakes of audience members.

Be flexible

Prepare more material than you can present, but do not try to include it all. Avoid content-driven presentations. Do not be so rigidly bound to a predetermined pattern of presentation. Prepare different approaches for presenting key points and then choose the approach that best suits the mood of your audience. For example, be prepared to switch off the projector if your audience is becoming bored with figures and graphs.

Encourage audience participation

Two-way communication is superior to one-way. It allows you to check audience understanding and raises their interest in your message by stimulating their curiosity. Be alert to possibilities for letting people in your audience act and speak. Ask 'friendly' questions, ask for volunteers to demonstrate, encourage the sharing of experiences to illustrate your point, use a visiting expert, and so on.

8 Practical exercises for employee training interventions

Exercise 1

Steve, a long-serving member of your staff, more often than not comes to work around 30 minutes late in the morning. You are the director of a very busy call-centre office and the phones start ringing promptly at 09:00 am. When he is late for work, you have to answer his phones and this interrupts your work tasks significantly. You think that it is time to put an end to that kind of attitude. One of your options is to threaten to fire him unless he shapes up. However, you cannot afford losing him because he is an extremely experienced, capable and high-performing worker. Currently, the company is facing some tough competition in the industry and it would be risky to lose him.

Task

In your group of learners, identify a list of approaches to solving this problem and discuss the advantages and disadvantages of each option. Then agree on a general strategy and list the specific steps you would take.

Exercise 2

Jonathan, the director of a well-known insurance company, scheduled a performance appraisal session with Robert, one of his insurance consultants, two hours ago. The discussion went as follows:

JONATHAN: Robert, I arranged this session because I want to talk about certain aspects of your work and my comments are not very favourable.
ROBERT: Sure Jonathan ... go ahead ... you are the boss!
JONATHAN: I think you create a poor impression to our clients because of appearance. A consultant is supposed to look more business-like. We

charge our clients a very high rate of service, so you cannot give them the impression that you do not have the money to buy good clothing.

ROBERT: I have little interest in trying to persuade my clients with my clothing ... besides, I have heard no complaints from them.

JONATHAN: I think that it matters a lot in our job. Anyway, let's talk about something else. I want to comment on the reports you prepare regarding our clients. They have many careless mistakes.

ROBERT: I have an increased workload, so I don't have much time to spend on writing more meticulous reports.

JONATHAN: By writing poor reports, you are causing me various problems. Nevertheless, another thing is that your office is a mess ... it is the worst-looking office in the company. Why can't you have a well-organised office?

ROBERT: What's the point of doing that? My clients never visit me at my office!

Task

In your group of learners, discuss how the interaction could have been changed to produce a better outcome. What principles of effective communication and listening are violated in this case?

Exercise 3

After a tremendous air-flight crash that you have survived, you find yourself on a small, deserted island that has no food or drinking water. Your location is unclear. You have managed to save an item of hand baggage, which contains six items undamaged.

Task

Rank the six items in terms of their importance for you, as you wait to be rescued. Place the number 1 by the most important item, the number 2 by the second-most important and so forth until you have ranked all six items.

Important note: First, you need to rank the items working on your own, and then you need to work as a team that should come to an agreement. You need to justify your arguments. You need to complete this team task strictly in 15 minutes.

Items:

1   A map of the Pacific Ocean
2   A shaving mirror
3   A 1-litre bottle of mineral water

4   An ocean fishing kit
5   A bar of chocolate
6   A small package of food (eked out, sufficient for 3 days).

[Answer: The main emphasis should be on items that can attract attention and aid survival until rescue arrives. Without signalling devices, there is almost no chance of being spotted and surviving. The shaving mirror is ranked 1st because it is the most powerful tool to attract attention since it can reflect light to a distance as far as the horizon and beyond. Next, you need water and food.]

Exercise 4

'Micropower' is a small high-tech firm that produces software programmes for corporations. It is run by a very enthusiastic and experienced owner. The company employs a general director, 15 full-time software design engineers (i.e. they design the programmes working individually at their offices) and five full-time IT consultants (i.e. they sell the programmes to the end-users, they train them on how to use the programmes, and they provide after-sales support and advice). All design engineers and consultants are well educated, whereas all consultants have a strong background and expertise in software engineering. The rewards are very generous within the firm (above the market average) with consultants getting a higher wage than software design engineers receive (i.e. £200 per month extra). In terms of staff training, there are frequent seminars for both consultants and designers in order to develop further their technical skills. Performance appraisal is conducted once a year by the general director based on a list of predetermined quantitative criteria (number of sales, number of programmes developed, etc.). Each year, the best software designer (according to performance evaluation) is given the opportunity for promotion to a consultancy role (thus earning a higher salary), whereas the best consultant gets a holiday package and a generous bonus. However, during the past year designers' productivity has declined significantly and this has caused serious problems for the firm.

Task

Based on case-study data, what can the general director do to improve staff performance? Discuss in teams what the main causes for the decline in staff productivity could be (e.g. any motivational issues). What action would you suggest? Suggest a list of measures and identify the advantages and disadvantages of each course of action.

Exercise 5

[This is an exercise that aims to help learners develop their problem-solving skills. In groups, the learners should complete the following open-ended questionnaire concerning their specific department in the organisation.]

Q1: Describe the change you wish to initiate (analyse the type of change, e.g. policy, structure, procedures, attitude)

_____

_____

_____

_____

Q2: Analyse your motives for promoting change

_____

_____

_____

_____

Q3: Describe why the organisation will benefit from this planned change

_____

_____

_____

_____

_____

Q4: Identify the forces that will promote or retard the introduction of this intended change (persons, situations, customs, etc.)

_____

_____

_____

_____

Q5: Make a list of the anticipative arguments that might be raised by those resistant to the change and outline how you can deflect its force

Arguments:

_____

_____

_____

_____

_____

Counter-arguments:

_____

_____

_____

_____

_____

Q6: What media will you use to communicate this message and to whom will you primarily direct this communication?

_____

_____

_____

_____

Q7: List the immediate steps to be taken to get the change accepted and functioning

_____

_____

_____

_____

Q8: Propose an alternative plan in case your initial plan is rejected

_____

_____

_____

_____

Exercise 6

[This is an exercise that aims to help learners develop their time-management, organisation and problem-solving skills. This is an individual task where the learners should complete the exercise strictly in 15 minutes.]

The following activity is a business simulation, where you play a member of staff who has to deal with the tasks of a busy day. You will be given a selection of letters, emails and notes, which somebody doing the job might find in their desk or email inbox first thing in the morning. You have to read each item, decide on the action to be taken and the priority to be allocated to it, and complete related tasks such as summarising a report or drafting a reply to an email. After reading the background of the situation, understanding the problem, and looking in your Inbox on your desk, you will have a series of decisions to make. Compile/organise your list of decisions in a document. There is no special format for creating the document as this exercise is designed for you to use your critical-thinking skills in a 'real life' decision-making exercise. In addition, you will reflect upon the decisions that you made and what you learnt about your decision-making approaches.

Background

You are Helen (or John) Stevens and you have been appointed to the position of Personal assistant to the General Director of a large European clothing company based in England manufacturing low-cost items for the domestic and international markets.

You arrived yesterday afternoon on Monday, 1st of March, and found that your predecessor, Jennifer Johnson, had already left to take up a position with another company. As a result you have not had the opportunity to discuss the current situation at the company with her. Since arriving yesterday, your time has been completely taken up with meeting staff (a list of key people is shown below) and familiarising yourself with the organisation.

Your problem

It is now 8.00 a.m. on Tuesday, 2nd of March, and in half an hour you must leave to go to London for an urgent personal matter and you are not scheduled to return until next Tuesday, 9th of March. There are a number of items that look as though they may need your attention before you leave for London. Some of these items seem to have been left by Mark Davis for you to handle.

Task

Go through all five items and note under each item whatever action you think seems necessary. Note down every action you would take and place them in a hierarchy.

Key personnel

- Chief Executive Officer: Mark Davis
- Personal assistant to CEO: '**You**!' (previously: Jennifer Johnson)
- General secretary: Demy Sue
- Production Manager: John Anderson
- Production Supervisor: Dennis Wilson
- Personnel and Public Relations manager: Anna Robins

(Item 1 – letter)
24 February
Dear Mr Davis
I hold 500 shares in your company and I have been concerned about the poor performance of the shares on the London Stock Exchange. The share price has not shown the growth that I hoped for and expected. I retired recently and I am very dependent on the performance of the shares I hold. Therefore, I would like to have a meeting with you at your earliest convenience to discuss what plans you have to improve the disappointing performance. I will telephone next week if I have not heard from you.

Yours sincerely,
Tony Smith

(Item 2 – email)
To: <Helen (or John) Stevens>
From: <Demy Sue>
Sent: 14:00 1 March
Subject: Absence
I am sorry I didn't mention it today, but I need to take Tuesday (tomorrow) off because I have an important appointment with my doctor. I thought I would be seeing you this afternoon, but didn't. I hope you don't mind. If you need me I can be contacted on my mobile phone. I hope this doesn't cause too much inconvenience.

Demy Sue
General Secretary

(Item 3 – memo)
Memo to: Mark Davis
From: Anna Robins
Date: 15 February
The Clothing Workers Union is pushing for some action on the new employment contract. The old agreement expired three months ago now. It is very clear that our ceiling of 2% on any wage increase and the proposed performance linked bonus will be the central issues given the rising rate of inflation.

There is considerable frustration among our workers and we need to move quickly if we want to avoid them giving notice of strike action. I can organise a meeting for next week, but we need to decide on how far we are prepared to move before we meet with the union.

(Item 4 – letter)
20 February
To: Mr Davis,
General Director
Dear Mr Davis
I am sorry that this is on such short notice, but I am herewith submitting my intention to resign after 15 years with the company. When I first began we treated our employees fairly and produced high quality products. During the last year, this has changed dramatically. I cannot continue to work in this line of thinking, so I wish to quit my job.

I am giving you three weeks' notice as required by my contract.

Yours sincerely,
Dennis Wilson

(Item 5 – note left on your desk yesterday)
Personal
I am sorry to have to leave before you start on the job. I am sure there are a number of things I am not able to bring you up to date on. Anyway, best of luck. I know you will do an excellent job.

I am sure you will get full co-operation from the staff. Don't hesitate to contact me via email if I can be of any help.

Best wishes
Jennifer Johnson

Exercise 7

'Phone Y' is a high-street mobile phone retailer in the UK. It has an extensive network of branches and also sells through a website. It operates in a highly competitive market place, competing with a host of smaller independent retailers. Depending on the size of outlet, a typical shop will employ between seven and ten full-time employees plus a manager. Each shop sells an almost bewildering array of phones. The company produces a monthly brochure summarising its best deals. Sales staff use a computer programme that prompts them to ask questions on customers' requirements, which then produces a list of recommended products and deals to choose from. Stores are set sales targets, and performance is measured against those targets and against the performance of similar stores. The company's software system records the number of enquiries handled by each member of staff, the proportion of enquiries that result in sales and the value of each sale. The company currently pays its sales staff on a standard hourly rate (based on the National Minimum Wage), with bonuses for meeting sales targets. The maximum bonus an individual is likely to receive will add 10 per cent to monthly wages. Only the top 50 per cent of sales staff receive any bonus at all. The hiring process is informal and based on application forms and structured interviews. Sales staff have a variety of educational backgrounds; however, most of them are further-education graduates. All newcomers attend a three-day formal sales-training seminar.

Problem

The company has grown aggressively over the last two years through new store openings. However, over the last eight months, sales in several existing stores have begun to stagnate and the company is not performing as well as its rivals. After careful analysis, the top executives of the company have realised that the causes of poor performance have been the poor financial rewards provided to sales staff, as well as their lack of competence.

Task

Create teams of two learners. The task of each team would be to prepare a 15-minute presentation on how sales could be improved in existing stores. The presentation should include specific recommendations for performance improvement.

Exercise 8

[The following exercise is an individual task particularly suitable for training workshops on managing stress at work.]

Task

Learners should identify all the key stressors for their job setting and family setting. They should then determine specific strategies to cope with stress. Their analysis should be written on paper and kept in their individual journals.

Exercise 9

'Fabritex' is an Italian, medium-sized textile organisation that produces fabrics for the domestic clothing market. The organisation has a very strict hierarchy. There are no women managers in the firm (all middle-level and senior management positions are occupied by males) due to the General Director's belief that all female workers are not career oriented. The company employs female workers only at the lower levels of the hierarchy (unskilled personnel) and offers them no access to training opportunities. There are frequent cases of sexual harassment (by senior staff), which are always ignored by the General Director of the firm. A month ago, a group of female workers complained formally to the owner of the organisation about the issue of gender discrimination. The owner listened carefully their claims and decided to appoint a new General Director in order to handle the major issue of gender inequality at work. The new Director, soon after his appointment, took the following measures:

- He created a new mission statement, which highlighted that the company would adopt a very strict gender equality policy
- He initiated a female internship programme to attract more women to the firm
- He took immediate action on the first case of sexual harassment through the imposition of a small fine to the male manager who was found guilty.

Despite all the above actions by the newly appointed Director, it has been a year and the situation has not been improved significantly. No women have been advanced to senior positions, whereas there are still cases of sexual harassment.

Task

In groups of two learners, discuss why the situation has not yet been improved within the firm. Then prepare an oral presentation outlining the actions that the newly appointed Director should take to eliminate the problem.

Exercise 10

'Food Z' is a small supermarket chain consisting of five shops in London. The company was established in 1990 and it is a family-run business. The supermarket cannot compete with the large supermarket chains on price, because it lacks the purchasing power, so the company has developed relationships with local suppliers and farmers, and prides itself on the quality and value for money of its products. Excellent customer service and friendliness is another aspect of the competitive strategy.

The shops

The shops all have the same basic organisational structure and offer the same range of goods. Each store employs 16 individuals: one store manager, one deputy manager, two security guards (working on a rota), two cleaners and ten part-time shop-floor employees working in very specific posts. The workers are paid the basic salary, whereas promotion is based on seniority. In terms of staff development, there is only very short initial training for all newcomers around health and safety, as well as on their main tasks. Most workers are young, high-school graduates (22–25 years old) with the rest being between 40 and 50 years old.

The problem

The shops have a good reputation for customer care and a good customer base. However, during the last year, they have been losing both staff and customers. Old and young employees are not relating well to one another, with older employees complaining about the lack of customer care young workers seem to have.

Task

In groups of two learners, discuss whether or not training could be the best way to solve the organisational problem faced by the company.

- If *yes*, prepare a short oral presentation on the types of training opportunities that 'Food Z' should offer its employees.
- If *no*, prepare a short oral presentation on the course of action that should be taken to improve firm performance (prepare a list of specific suggestions with full justification).

Concluding remarks

The main objective of this text has been to explore the process of employee training in large and small organisations, as well as examine the factors determining training provision in such establishments. In this closing chapter, a number of key conclusions are drawn based on the points raised throughout the book.

First, it is important for managers to understand that there are substantial problems in ascertaining any causal link between staff training and business performance. To put it simply, the task of identifying a causal relationship between training and firm performance seems futile. Managers place too much blind trust in employee training. For example, there is a myth that training has always had a direct impact on productivity, so it should not be subject to the same budgetary constraints as other expenditures. However, productivity improvement stems from a far more complex process. Training is just one factor in productivity improvement. For training to be effective, managers need to separate symptoms from 'trainable problems'. Training may offer various other non-measurable benefits to employees but it is important to fit it into the specific corporate culture of an organisation. It is also more appropriate to identify and stress the positive outcomes from training interventions that are advantageous for organisations in the widest sense, rather than seeking to demonstrate causal relationships.

Furthermore, it is important to point out that formal training is not the single most important factor towards skills upgrading of employees. As it is argued in this book, learning in the day-to-day work environment appears to be a very good way for organisations to meet any skill shortages and maximise their organisational effectiveness. It should be recognised that learning within organisations is often informal and incidental, and facilitated by managers, supervisors and peers. Employees develop a range of skills from their everyday experiences in informal ways, which means that many firms do not want or need to adopt more-formal approaches to learning.

In terms of the determinants of training in companies, it should be noted that the training activity is influenced by a host of factors including the owner's commitment towards employee learning and knowledge sharing, the competitive strategies adopted by organisations, management support, skill shortages in the external labour market, the way work practices are designed and financial constraints. Trainers and HR managers need to be aware of all these factors since they tend to affect the nature, extent and impact of training provision.

Last but not least, it should be stressed that nowadays HR managers need to train their employees in order to develop a range of 'soft' skills. In the past, skill used to be equated with the 'hard' technical abilities and 'know-how' of the skilled manufacturing worker or the analytical capacities of the scientist or technician. Today, 'skill' is altogether more perplexing and includes a range of personal qualities that employees need to develop in order to be able to contribute towards the achievement of organisational objectives.

Further reading

DeSimone, R. L., Werner, J. M. and Harris, D. M. (2002) *Human Resource Development,* 3rd edn. Fort Worth, TX: Harcourt College Publishers.

Evans, K., Hodkinson, P. and Unwin, L. (2002) *Working to Learn.* London: Routledge.

Harrison, R. (2009) *Learning and Development,* 5th edn. London: CIPD.

Stewart, J. and McGoldrick, J. (1996) *Human Resource Development: Perspectives, Strategies and Practice.* London: Pitman.

Stone, R. J. (2002) *Human Resource Management,* 4th edn. Australia: John Wiley and Sons.

Index